AUTHOR'S NOTE

I was somewhat frail and small as a child, an introverted bookworm, and was early dubbed a weakling by my peers, arousing all sorts of problems.

I was also a psychic child, which itself aroused problems of all kinds, but which somewhat accounts for my long-prevailing and dedicated interest in psychical matters.

Despite many hardships and disappointments, in my own estimation, I've lived a good, fulfilling, and even wonderful life and I'm in no way displeased with any of it...and all in all, I've actually done most of what I've wanted to do, which is somewhat more than many can say, and I'm content in this.

I'm older now, and have begun the slide into old age and set about writing culminations of what I fondly refer to as "my life's works," of which this book is one.

INGO SWANN
NEW YORK

Ingo Swann (1933-2013) was an American artist and exceptionally successful subject in parapsychology experiments.

As a child he spontaneously had numerous paranormal experiences, mostly of the OBE type, the future study of which became a major passion as he matured. In 1970, he began acting as a parapsychology test subject in tightly controlled laboratory settings with numerous scientific researchers. Because of the success of most of these thousands of test trials, major media worldwide often referred to him as "the scientific psychic." His subsequent research on behalf of American intelligence interests, including that of the CIA, won him top PSI-spy status.

His involvement in government research projects required the discovery of innovative approaches toward the actual realizing of subtle human energies. He viewed PSI powers as only parts of the larger spectrum of human sensing systems and was internationally known as an advocate and researcher of the exceptional powers of the human mind.

To learn more about Ingo, his work, art, and other books, please visit: **www.ingoswann.com.**

PRESERVING
the
psychic child

A BioMind Superpowers Book
Published by

Swann-Ryder Productions, LLC
www.ingoswann.com

First edition BioMind Superpowers Books.
ISBN-13: 978-1-949214-40-6

Cover art: **Take Care** by Ingo Swann
© Swann-Ryder Productions, LLC

Internal art: Shutterstock.com

Light Bulbs in Hand © Igor Shi
Childhood © NadzeyaShanchuk
Silhouette of Children on White Background © Nowik Sylwia
Open Door in Universe © intueri
Influencer © Juergen Priewe
Collector © Juergen Priewe
Woman's and Child's Handprints © Eva Speshneva
Realistic Hand or Palm Print © CoffeeTime
Window Cleaners Wash Universe © intueri
Paper Plane Dreams to Become the Big Plane © intueri
Follow Dreams © intueri
Open Blue Door and Sunshine © Elena Schweitzer
Space Badge with Spilled Universe © Sloth Astronaut
Happy Children Pupils Jumping with School Bell © Valenty
Happy Jumping Children Holding Hands © Valenty
Hand Holding Puzzle © Anttoniart
Boy and the Old Man Go to Eternity © intueri

PRESERVING
the
psychic child

INGO SWANN

PUBLISHER'S NOTE

Implied in the following text is Ingo Swann's notion that one should look not at words as words but rather as vessels that carry meanings, and relationships of meanings.

Started by Ingo in the late 1980s and extending into the early 1990s, this work appears to be a contemplation for Ingo, a reflection on his own experiences as a child – experiences that would form the groundwork for all that he would later become.

Thus with great elation, it is our pleasure to share **Preserving the Psychic Child**, Ingo's previously unpublished work, with the world.

for my sisters
MARLYS AND MURLEEN

TABLE OF CONTENTS

FRONT MATTER

"Truth is ever to be found in simplicity, and not in the multiplicity and confusion of things."

-- ISAAC NEWTON

OPENING THOUGHTS

I was born in the early morning hours of September 14, 1933, delivered by the town doctor of Telluride, Colorado, in an upstairs bedroom of my maternal grandmother's home. It was only years later that I realized a memory of the birth sequence existed somewhere within me: a recall of an intense pressure, dark, distorting the whole body, painless, then a burst of light exploding in my head. A light that was nothing more than the light bulb hanging in the room, but to my blank brain, and its light-sensitive synapses, it was a flood of painful brilliance, my eyes for the first time processing light signals. Too much light so suddenly, when perhaps babies should birth into semi-darkness to prevent such intense light flooding.

For my mother, it was, I later learned, an ordeal. I was a little late in coming and was a big baby, weighing in at nine pounds. It was an event, for I was the first grandchild on both sides of the family, born into a clan of various aunts and uncles, all of whom had grown up with each other in the small confines of Telluride – a clan that was to lavish attention upon me for the years of infancy.

When I was but a small infant, the "I" part of me was often not within my little body, but rather was outside of it, watching and experiencing the vast amounts of emotion and love that were poured in at it.

I can say, I remember numerous details from this period, the color of blankets in the small crib on wheels my mother pulled through the house to keep me near her at all times, the two strings of beads, one blue, one pink, she used to entertain me, the warmth of the stove in the kitchen and the one between the dining and living rooms.

Of course, no one else suspected this out-of-body condition, and I had no real understanding of it until some thirty years later when I was finally able to understand it for what it had been. This out-of-body component was to erupt and become problematical to all concerned barely two and a half years later when I could talk enough to begin telling of out-of-body experiences to a totally unsuspecting family and clan of aunts and uncles.

My family might have been prepared for the hard life, but they were not prepared for a clairvoyant child who began to narrate the fabled out-of-body condition to them, perplexing and confusing all involved.

While some might doubt that one can have memories of one's own birth and the first three months of life, these memories exist in deeper levels of our psychic structures where the effects are much the same, whether the memories are consciously accessible or not. This is generally accepted now in psychology as there is even a clear reality that the child experiences, and is marked, by many things – emotions and events – while still being carried within the mother.

All this implies, I think, is that there is something we should call the psychic environment, a telepathic environment that exists along with the physical realm. It is into this psychic environment that love creates energy and underwrites the many positive expressions of life that follow because of it. Regardless of whatever tribulations that existed in my childhood, I had no doubt at all that I was loved.

***

My own cultural imprinting consisted, in large part, of the basic approaches to a hard life. But the frontier traditions of Telluride of the early 1930s that I was born into deeply affected me also, as did the natural beauty and wonders of the mountain surroundings.

It was this natural magnificence, together with its unpredictable dangers and calamities, I believe, that installed in me a perpetual sense of struggle and survival-triumph, and built within me a preference for the heroic, the cosmic and the profound along with a connection to, and appreciation for, nature's beauty.

I believe that cultural imprintings are vibrations that once set in motion in childhood, never leave the spirit-body combination out of which we are all developed.

My cultural imprinting has several layers on the human side of things, which, in my retrospection now at the age of fifty-two, I can see as somewhat diametrically opposed to the heroic-cosmic-profound imprinting.

As children, we cannot help but take on the values, for better or worse, of our family and the people around us, their hopes, aspirations, prejudices, and goals and traditions.

However opposing some of these many factors might be, the child eventually makes a synthesis of them – a synthesis that might be benevolently comfortable and constructive, or a mess and defective in the long run, or anywhere in between these two poles.

Our cultural imprinting sinks into our unconscious as we grow up and is overlaid with new values from where, unknown to our conscious awarenesses, it invokes a sort of hypnotic influence over many of our preferences and actions throughout life.

INTRODUCTION:
PRESERVING THE PSYCHIC CHILD

In this small book, I've drawn together some of the most important features of the psychic child.

Parents, sensing that these qualities somehow are the foundations for several of the child's other attributes, may seek to preserve their child's psychic qualities.

Preservation requires a good grasp of the child's fundamental psychic nature; only through this kind of understanding can constructive help and guidance can be undertaken.

There is nothing in this book that is difficult or complex. In fact, once the basic issues are grasped, the child's psychic abilities can be preserved through the use of common sense.

***

I was born a psychic child – one who was also very precocious and strong-willed. But I was born into a family, and more so, into a small-town society, that had little comprehension about anything psychic. Because of this, my parents and the society I was born into, could not value the psychic qualities of an infant or child.

This was not particularly the fault of my family members or of society. It was more the fault of the system into which they had been born and had to function. Nothing in their education had prepared them to understand my basic psychic nature, or deal with a child who became psychically active at a very early age.

For them, and for me, it was a very rough road. And in the end, the norms of society won out. By the time I had spent two years in grade school, all of my psychic abilities had been forced to introvert. These abilities did not reemerge until forty years later, at the time I began participating in formal parapsychology experiments.

Since then, I've worked with numerous important research centers doing hundreds of thousands of experiments with people devoted to discovering the mysterious elements of the psychic realm.

Almost from the beginning of my adult work, I realized how significant my psychic childhood had been. I came to understand that no one can achieve anything unless the rudiments and foundations of their achievements are already in place within them.

Through the last fifteen years, I've collected a large dossier about the child's psychic nature and the close connection of that nature to the child's future creative potentials. In my opinion, all the issues involved have been made to seem far more complex than they really are.

This short compilation is offered as a help to the parent who might be mystified about the child's behavior – and to the child, once they are old enough to read what is contained herein.

Although I lean heavily on my own childhood experiences to support my conclusions, I owe a great debt to many other sensitive researchers who have explored the basic nuisances of both the psychic child as well as the creative child.

It is their work that has helped give substance to my own experiences and deductions.

INTRODUCTION:
INTO THE PSYCHIC REALM

et us begin with common sense. Almost everyone will agree that if you want something to grow, it has to be nourished. And in order to nourish it properly, you have to understand this thing's basic properties so as to figure out its nourishment needs.

Take an apple tree for example, the apple seedling is nourished through nature because it is going to grow into a tree and produce apples.

The human being is, of course, much more complicated, but the analogy is appropriate. Children are nourished because they are going to grow into adults and produce their contributions to the human burden of life.

If the child does this well, they fulfill themselves.

If the child doesn't, they occupy much the same place as does the tree that produces malformed or rotten apples.

Proper nourishment is a common-sense law of life for all things that grow. But if the apple tree and the human being both need nourishment, they are, in other ways, obviously quite different.

Apple seedlings grow up to become standard apple trees.

Children do not grow up to become standard adults, instead children grow up with wonderful powers of transformation that help them to develop along the way.

The apple tree cannot transform itself into

anything other than an apple tree. Human beings, with their powers of transformation, can become many, many different kinds of adults. A child's growth and success is reflected through their powers of creativity, genius, leadership, and human and spiritual sensitivity.

These incredible qualities, seen within growth, all bestow magnificent powers of transformation, and produce the brilliantly diverse products that ennoble the human race.

These powers of transformation begin with the child, and each power must receive nourishment, very early, because if these powers don't, they might wither away.

At the bottom of almost all of the transformative abilities of the individual is human and spiritual sensitivity.[1]

And beneath sensitivity is one fundamental human potential that has so far not received nearly enough attention: this is the psychic realm, a far broader foundation that supports and gives vital energies to sensitivity.

All the available evidence tells us that the psychic realm is part and parcel of the child's experience. The child is born with it, and participates in it, long before learning anything else.

This psychic realm is first encountered by the mother. Most mothers know there is a telepathic link between them and their child.

Awareness of this telepathic link often begins while the mother is still carrying the child. Sometimes it lasts into the child's mature life.

---

[1] The insensitive individual is locked out of much of the life experience that is available to others in whom sensitivity has been well nourished.

The child experiences it, too.

This telepathic link is direct evidence for a far larger psychic realm, with which the child also has extensive contacts.

This mysterious realm is invisible and not very well understood. Consequently, this mysterious realm's manifestations can appear strange and uncanny to those who don't know what to expect.

But this same realm is closely connected to one of humankind's highest attributes: intuition.

And, in turn, intuition is closely connected to transformative powers of creativity, genius, leadership, and human and spiritual sensitivity.

The law of nourishment tells our common sense, then, that if the child's psychic potential is not understood and nourished, it will probably not be preserved and with that, many of the transformative powers depending on it may wither and completely disappear.

To understand and preserve the psychic child is to give life to many of the child's other capabilities.

PART **ONE**

"In today's advancing understanding of human psychology, the most important and sensitive time for us, happens in the first few years of childhood."

-- INGO SWANN

THE PSYCHIC CHILD
AND THE CHILD PSYCHIC

There appear to be two basic types of psychic children.

Some seem to have only a passing connection with their psychic capabilities: their gift quickly sinks beneath the level of their other awarenesses and interests. Such children are far in the majority. Their psychic potentials have receded to their roots, there to help fortify in unconscious ways, their other more conscious aptitudes – intuition, hunches, creativity. Their psychic elements never intrude themselves, and many adults go through life without even being aware they have a psychic level of awareness.

The other type of psychic children are those who show marked tendencies toward being psychic. They start using their psychic potentials very early. They start talking about their psychic awarenesses, and ask questions about them.

Sometimes one or more of their awarenesses grow into distinct abilities or talents. These children become very good at extrasensory perception, or other types of psychic activities. With these children, the psychic child becomes the child psychic.

The difference between these two basic types revolves around orientation, emphasis, and activity.

Identifying the distinction between the two serves to establish a kind of reference system, allowing parents to see which pole their child is nearest to.

Between the two poles exists a vast variety of psychic children.

THE EMERGING
PSYCHIC CHILD

After the baby is born, it isn't very long before the infant begins to take an interest in the world all around – a luminous world, full, quite different from the prenatal environment. The little machine begins its amazing functioning, and the child is launched into life.

Despite our thinking to the contrary, the child's psychic state is not automatically closed down when the physical sense organs and post-natal consciousness begin to operate.

Psychic abilities remain.

There is some evidence that the undefinable perceptions of the psychic state merge with the now developing perceptions of the physical machine.

For example, babies have been observed apparently watching things others cannot see.

Other times, parents sneak quietly into the nursery, not wanting to wake the sleeping child, only to find their child awake and already watching the door, as if the child were expecting the parents.

With the majority of children, it is clear that the psychic state does close down eventually, or that it is submerged beneath the more powerful physical senses.

When this happens, the psychic state is destined never to reemerge except in those rare instances when, usually as an adult, the individual spontaneously experiences a strange psychic encounter of some kind.

Some children, though, remain in a psychic state for quite some time.

When this happens, the parents and family find themselves confronted by a psychic child who is apparently living in two distinct universes: the objective universe of the senses; and the invisible universe of the psychic state. Moreover, not only does the psychic state prolong itself, it begins to develop.

The child appears to be using the psychic state as an additional method, accompanying the child's normal senses, to interpret the world around them.

This situation usually becomes apparent after the child has learned enough of the language to begin talking about and describing things the parents cannot see or understand.

Often the child reports "seeing" not only the physical bodies of things, but the lights and energies (auras) around them. Sometimes the child develops a distinct ability to locate things the child cannot have possibly seen – for example, toys that the parents have hidden because they might be dangerous to the infant.

Sometimes the child clearly anticipates the parent, as if the child is reading the parent's thoughts.

And, sometimes, the child says that they can "see" what the parent is thinking.

Eventually, some children begin to play and commune with unseen "friends," who may be anything from obvious fantastic constructions – miniature pink elephants, perhaps – to well-defined spirit-like "people" with names.

There have been occasions when such "people" turned out to be a deceased grandparent or other family relation the child had not yet heard about.

It is at this point, especially if the phenomena continue, that problems begin.

The parents naturally expect that, under their guidance, the child will develop normally, and will tend toward a uniformity with other children. They intend that their child's behavior shall be socially correct.

The psychic child, however, has become uncanny.

The parent who has no knowledge, at all, about things psychic will naturally feel that the child has to be corrected.

If the psychic element of the child has grown strong, the child will try to resist this corruption. The child's psychic impressions are just as real to them as anything else is, perhaps more so.

Such a situation will almost always result in confrontations, traumatic both for the child and the parents.

It has been observed that if the child's psychic tendencies are left alone, the child will eventually integrate them into their general developing interests in the outer world, where they tend ultimately to disappear – simply because, as the child develops, the outer world becomes more complex, and its issues take precedence.

In the normal course of the parent-child relationship, the parents have no idea how to react to a manifest psychic situation. They usually opt for the tried-and-true method of bringing force upon the child to abandon all these uncanny attributes.

TWO BASIC QUALITIES

OF THE PSYCHIC CHILD

It must be admitted frankly that no one knows exactly what role the psychic element plays in the child's development.

Such development's inner workings are quite invisible and beyond rational explanation.

Yet, the parents who take an interest in their child's overall education can, by assisting the child's psychic growth, come to realize that they are playing a very important part in their child's overall development.

One of the most interesting facts about the psychic child is that the psychic element is, at first, simply a state of existence, as the mother-child telepathic bonding shows.

The child is in natural rapport with the mother, and often with other family members.

Some psychic children, a few years after their

birth, claim they have invisible friends, *beings* with whom they talk and play.

This is another type of telepathic bonding. They are in natural rapport with these invisible beings.

When questioned about the being's identity, the child will often ask it, that question, and return an answer.

When the child is challenged with the idea that the invisible being does not exist, the child will become very defensive.

This stage of life, if left to follow its own course, normally peters out, as the child replaces these earlier bonds with other, stronger ones.

There can be little doubt that the psychic child is sensing things outside the immediate confines of the child's own physical body.

As this telepathic bonding extends into the environment, it becomes a natural condition of existence: very soon the child is using their telepathic bond as a tool to gather information. Because of this, the psychic child probably experiences, to some degree, the feelings and emotions of those with whom it has a telepathic link.

If parents understand and expect telepathic linking, the overall well-being of the family unit takes on a greater importance than ever before.

If the family unit is linked psychically, the infant is sharing, at its psychic level, the pains and pleasures of the family members.

PART **TWO**

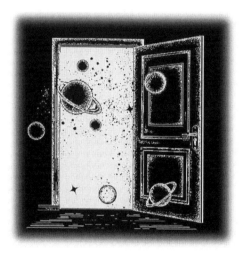

"Even though this world is narrow, it is wide...to those who understand.

This world isn't the only one."

-- CLAMP

THE BACKGROUND
OF THE PSYCHIC CHILD

People give a lot of attention to what is visible. However, everything in the universe has both visible and invisible parts. Even rocks contain invisible energies that we can't see. Coal, for example, is a hard, black substance. But it contains energies that can be released as heat when it burns.

When the child is born, the child comes equipped with many invisible attributes besides the little body visible to everyone.

The little body of the baby is its visible aspect. Inside this body, though, many invisible processes are already working, especially those involving its ability to learn things. This is because they need to *know* a lot about the invisible so that they can come to understand the processes through which the invisible energies and forces work.

The child has both visible and invisible parts, and we can call these levels, because the differences between them can be measured, and because each one needs to be understood differently from the others.

All the levels taken together constitute the background of the psychic child. They each hold a different natural endowment the child comes with.

So that the natural endowment these levels contain can be developed, each level needs to be understood and nourished.

THE FIRST LEVEL:
PHYSICAL BODY AND PRIMAL INDIVIDUALITY

The child's physical body and their individuality comprise the first level.

The child is a physical bundle of joy for the parents and family. But the child is born physically helpless, cooing and crying with radiant and inquisitive eyes.

These little eyes busy themselves trying to take in everything that abounds.

The little baby is born loving the parents. This invisible bond is one of the first things that becomes established.

The child is bundled up and carried around with pride.

The child is nursed and cared for, often to the exhaustion of the parents.

The parents begin to plan for the child's future. They create this future in their own image, often with the desire to make sure the child has everything the parents did not have.

It is only natural to plan that this future will be a normal one.

But lo – the baby, helpless in so many things, very early makes its own personality and individuality apparent.

The individuality of the new baby, especially if it is an only child, might not be grasped very quickly by the parents. But those who have more than one child, rapidly come to recognize qualities that make the child distinctive. Parents may quickly come to realize that they cannot serve only as role models for the rapidly developing infant – they must accommodate the individuality of the child as well.

They discover that the baby has not only physical needs, but emotional needs as well. And before very long, the child's intellectual needs also show themselves too.

If all of these needs are relatively consistent with what the parents have to offer, the communal growth of parents and child proceeds apace. If not, the parents quickly begin to feel the stress.

Today, more than ever in the past, there are many valuable resources for parents to draw upon. Parents are increasingly aware that the infant stage is one of primary importance, and many are learning how easy it is to set aside their own preconceptions of what they want their child to become.

The new-age parent, especially, accepts that

the child should not be forced to mold itself in the image of the parents. But all parents do come to realize that the child is a different being from themselves.

Upbringing is a matter of cooperation and guidance.

The most productive kind of upbringing is one that does not force the child into a mold for which the child might be unsuited or unfitted.

Such an upbringing takes into account how the child is different from the child's parents as well as how the child is alike.

THE SECOND LEVEL:

THE LITTLE MACHINE AND ITS GROWING AND LEARNING PROCESSES

eneath the first level of the child, truly amazing things are taking place. With birth, the physical sense organs of the infant are brought into contact with the elements of the outer world.

The little body is also like a little engine that takes up the enormous work of processing everything in the outer world around it.

Sound waves, light, shadows, darkness, shapes, forms, all these inundate the little engine. It begins the formidable work of making sense of all these things. And it does so in a remarkably short period of time.

The little engine is one of inconceivable delicacy.

With astonishing rapidity, it grows, changes size and shape and performs ever more involved operations.

This little engine becomes more and more sensitive, and performs more and more complex activities, in answer to more and more complex influences around it.

Responsiveness increases; its experiences multiply. Soon the little engine is doing more than any conceivable engine could.

The little engine is recreating the universe around it inside itself, an astonishing and sublime feat.

Yet even all this is not enough. It is getting ready to perform feats even more extraordinary.

Suddenly, one day, it begins to create its own language. At first, only the rudiments show up. These rudiments are common to all babies on earth.

The parents quickly help the child identify which language it should learn.

And by the time the baby is three, the little machine speaks.

Behind all this, in the little machine, a series of infinitesimal thought processes are at work. We soon take them for granted. But they utterly boggle scientific researchers who are trying to find out about them.

The parents and family see them as cute. But beneath their totally enjoyable cuteness, a formidable cosmic activity is in the process of fulfilling itself.

Sometimes, parents lose contact with their child at this point – especially if the emerging capabilities of the little machine are too far outside expectation.

For example, once in a while a child develops a language of two thousand words before they can even walk well. Some children can use eight thousand words by the time they are four. This is the normal vocabulary of an average mature individual.

The little machine often begins to ask questions parents can't answer or don't want to answer. The first real crisis ensues.

The little machine continues to develop anyway.

Scientists today are now coming into a more intimate comprehension that the mind of the little machine, even in its very first months, is the furnace in which the future adult is being forged.

Abilities, interests, and talents are all being formed at the very earliest stages. The early experiences will profoundly shape everything.[2]

The infant's brain is neither a blank slate nor a miniature form of the adult's brain.

It is a superactive system in which trillions of neurons and interconnecting nerve fibers are getting ready to explode into ever-increasing activity, to blossom and transfigure the infant in many different directions.

How all this happens remains something of a profound mystery, but it is known that as the integrations proceeds, any experiences the child may have can alter the brain's performances for

---

[2] Researchers are studying the developmental processes of the infant's brain for clues about how learning experiences originate and develop, while others are studying behavior.

better or for worse.

As amazing as all this is, most parents become aware that beneath all this spontaneous development of the little machine there is something else.

THE THIRD LEVEL:
THE BEING INSIDE

It isn't long after birth before the parent is forced to realize one thing: inside the little machine is a joyful, but observing, calculating intellect. The parents expect this – but it is an awesome event when it becomes apparent.

The modern scientific world – based in materialism – calls it an intellect. But the world of the soul has always preferred the term being.

In either case, the little engine slowly, by imperceptible steps, transforms itself from the state of mere infancy, through that of a little machine, into that of an intellect-being.

Inside the little machine is a being of intelligence which is transforming itself from one order of perception, thought, and action to a higher one.

This intellect-being is already possessed of qualities entirely of its own.

Neither the immediate environment nor the parents, can put those qualities there.

We now witness a phenomenon that confuses many parents.

If the little machine is indeed little, needing help to develop, the intellect-being is not little at all, and does not need help.

It needs guidance.

Even at birth, this intellect-being is rather well defined and bears delicate, but definite traits and characteristics of its own.

The parents who view the child as merely a physical extension of their own bodies are in for trouble – and the child is in for trauma.

The success of the family group rises and falls on this issue.

The sensitivities of the parents, and their alertness, to the different kinds of help and guidance that each level requires, will, in large part, shape the life of their child.

THE FOURTH LEVEL:
THE BEING'S PSYCHIC AWARENESS

he intellect-being inside the little machine reaches out with invisible feelers; this is the psychic infant.

The ability of the infant to reach out psychically cannot – and should not – be denied.

The telepathic bond between the child and the mother is the form in which this ability is most frequently encountered, and is very pronounced, and in fact, the scientific evidence for it is substantial.

But there is also a telepathic bond between the child and the father and telepathic bonding between siblings; that between twins in particular has been amply demonstrated.

With apparently little effort, the psychic infant can make its needs and wants known to the mother. Her own telepathic threshold might be too low to allow a response except in moments of crisis and danger to the child. Almost all mothers will respond then. This particular telepathic bond often lasts throughout life. Many mothers know when their child has been injured or killed in battle halfway around the world, for example.

The psychic infant quickly grows into the psychic child. The intellect-being reaches out into the universe. The psychic infant perceives things beyond the normal capabilities of the physical senses. The child, later, often mentions them, to the consternation of the family.

The psychic child intuits, sees through physical things, perceives strange energies and colors, communes with invisible beings, and sometimes foretells the future.

The psychic child sometimes remembers past lives and, in rare cases, knows who the parents or siblings were in a past life also.

The child knows, at a distance, where things are, and how relatives are doing.

The psychic child exhibits an astonishing array of facts and knowledge the child could not have acquired in their limited span of life.

Sometimes the psychic child demonstrates high-stage complicated talents of a magnitude so complex that it would normally take a lifetime to acquire them. These children are called child wizards or prodigies.

It is apparent that psychic abilities and intellectual giftedness are closely associated, at least in early childhood.

Child geniuses are limited only by the slow growth of their bodies. Still, the world has recognized them in all walks of life – in mathematics, music, art, sports, science, and invention.

But the psychic arts and talents are among life's least understood attributes. The psychic child will suffer horribly if the parents are not alert and responsive to these elusive gifts.

PART **THREE**

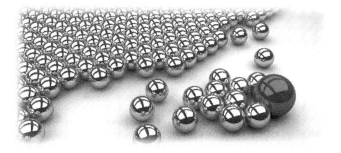

"As I review the events of my past life I realize how subtle are the influences that shape our destinies."

-- **NIKOLA TESLA**

THE CHILD'S
PSYCHIC STATE

Many mothers have experienced the strange phenomenon of being quite certain they are in some kind of communion with their child while the child is still in their own body.

This implies that the child's psychic abilities become functional before the child is born. They are automatically linked to those of the mother, although the mother's own psychic nature may have become completely introverted as she matured.

But during the gestation of her child, her own psychic nature is automatically resurrected, and the child-mother link is set up.

This implies that the prenatal infant, the little body still forming inside the mother, is possessed before its birth with some type of conscious awareness. This awareness, in turn, is built upon some kind of psychic base that grants the infant communion with the universe around it before it is born.

If this supposition is accepted, then many things that have always mystified everyone about the child psychic and the mature psychic must now be looked at differently.

This means that psychic giftedness is not a product of conscious awareness and education or study, as is generally thought. Such thinking places the cart before the horse. Rather, conscious awareness is built upon the psychic state and the psychic state originates in the prenatal condition.

This is a shocker! But it explains many things.

It explains why the mother-child telepathic bonding remains strong. It explains the father-child telepathic bonding, and especially the telepathic bonding of twins. All these bondings began before the child began the actual birth experience and became a little machine in its own right.

The best definition of a psychic whether child or adult – is of a person who is in touch with all things through some kind of mysterious energy that is invisible and intangible to the normal physical senses.

The psychical perceptions by which the child makes this communication are undefinable and imperceptible.

If after birth the child remains in contact with these undefinable perceptions, the child will be what is commonly thought of as a child psychic.

If an adult recontacts them, rehabilitates them through chance or willpower, that adult will become an adult psychic.

THE CHILD'S
CONSCIOUS AND UNCONSCIOUS AWARENESS

he foregoing picture would be incomplete if we did not add to it the idea of unconscious awareness.

These days it is generally accepted by science that even when an individual loses consciousness, some kind of non-conscious perceptions continue to function.

Evidence for this suggestion comes from people who have been anesthetized for surgery, or have been made unconscious through hypnosis or through clinical death experiences which they have survived.

Ordinary sleep is a type of unconsciousness, yet almost everyone knows that all sorts of perceptions continue to function during it.

Many mature psychic mediums – such as Edgar Cayce and Eileen Garrett – functioned only when they were in a type of unconsciousness.

Their everyday consciousness, their physical senses, were suspended. They re-submerged themselves into the realm of unconscious awareness in which enormous amounts of information were available to them.

In this state, these individuals delivered information that they could not possibly have obtained through normal conscious means.

It is quite probable that a fetus exists in a state of unconsciousness, at least as far as its physical sensory organs are concerned. But the fetus's unconscious (psychic) perceptions may be active, and if so, if its contact with the universe is anywhere near the magnitude of the well-developed, adult medium's – such as Edgar Cayce – then the fetus' access to information must be enormous.

So the implication is that the unborn child shares – at the very least – the experiences and conditions of the mother and those of the other people with whom it has established primary telepathic bonds. But it may have psychic access to a great deal of other information as well.

This recalls old wives' tales that a bad experience suffered by the pregnant mother can mark the child for life.

Upon this building block of unconscious and conscious psychic awarenesses are constructed the child's future learning capabilities, intellect, and overall awareness.

The infant's psychic phase is, therefore, of great importance.

PART **FOUR**

"Wise rising gives joy."

-- EGYPTIAN PROVERB

CONSERVING
THE PSYCHIC CHILD

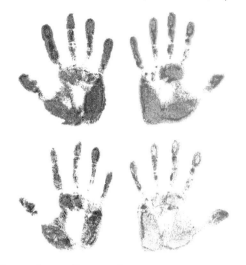

he only really good reason for preserving or conserving something is because it has a value of some kind. Anything that is meant to grow also needs help and guidance to develop.

Preserve means to keep from injury, harm, or destruction. And conserve means to keep in a safe, sound state. Conserving the psychic child means providing the child's psychic elements with nourishment.

In our apple tree example, if you injure the roots of the apple seedling, the tree will not grow very well.

***

The two most easily accepted psychic phenomena are telepathic bonding and intuition.

These are accepted because they are experienced by many people.

Telepathic bonding is important because it gives one a sense of unity and belonging with others.

Intuition is important because of its close connection with creativity and inventiveness.

Both telepathic bonding and intuition are related to human sensitivity. And without sensitivity, child or adult can become a beast who acts in uncaring and destructive ways.

The child's psychic nature acts as roots for these two qualities, and, as with the apple seedling, if these roots are damaged, then the child's inventiveness, creativity, intuition, and sense of bonding will not flourish very well.

The psychic child cannot easily be preserved without knowing how the child's psychic state or developing psychic talents fit in with the other aspects of the child's life.

The best general plan to preserve the psychic child is to have a good idea of how the child's psychic traits fit in with other aspects of the child's development.

The goal should be to attain harmony and balance by encouraging the child's psychic nature to take its appropriate place among the child's other attributes.

THE PSYCHIC GIFTEDNESS

OF THE CHILD

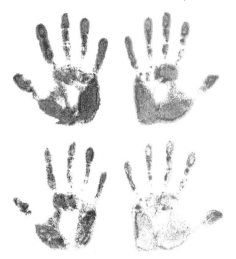

If the infant's natural psychic gift doesn't recede beneath the welter of conscious activities, but begins instead to push itself forward, the active child psychic has emerged.

The course of the psychic child's development depends at first almost solely on how the parents and immediate family respond to the child.

A little later, when the child begins to live beyond the family circle, the child's course will be further affected by teachers and relationships with peers.

It is perhaps not necessary to state that if the child encounters abundant anti-psychic hostility along the way, the child will be deeply marked, in an invisible and indelible fashion.

Since our society rejects the reality of psychic experience, its forced disappearance in the child will be welcomed by the child's parents, teachers, and peers, regardless of the cost to the child.

If the child persists in being psychic, therefore, the best thing would be to consider the psychic element as a form of giftedness – of potential genius.

In fact, it is becoming increasingly clear that genius rests upon a strong psychic foundation.

The reminiscences and autobiographical notes of many highly creative and inventive people contain reflections that aptly illustrate this connection.

For example, geniuses such as Albert Einstein, Nikola Tesla, Freud, and Jung all show, distinctly, the psychic processes that led to their major discoveries.

The steam engine was seen in a vision by its inventor, as was the cotton gin.

The works of major artists usually have a psychic source of inspiration, such as the psychic-style event that led Michelangelo to the concept of the Sistine ceiling.

The evidence for the close connection between the enhanced psychic state and all types of creativity has grown to such proportions that it can hardly be ignored any longer.

Psychic giftedness is not altogether different from other forms of giftedness or super-giftedness, except that it concerns a realm of human potential that our present science-oriented society has branded *suspect*.

Although psychic giftedness was valued by premodern societies, the world has just passed through a phase in which an elusive interest in the physical and material has dominated all else. This lopsided outlook has proved damaging to studies of the human being's many invisible attributes.

Psychic giftedness is different from other forms of giftedness in quality. But it shares the special learning problems and difficulties common to all forms.

GIFTED
IN A MULTIPLE WAY

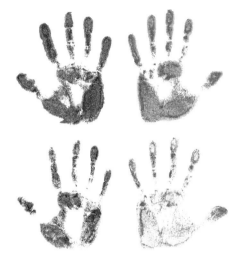

Some psychic children will be gifted in a multiple way. They demonstrate a marked superiority over average children. Because of their wide-ranging interests, they have a tendency to be robust and healthy, with a broad outlook. They often investigate a lot of different studies concurrently.

The psychic giftedness of those in this general group may easily go unnoticed at first. If their giftedness is not reinforced, the child might allow these attributes to submerge very early, because their interest in other things, which are reinforced instead, will take precedence.

The child will naturally allow their psychic abilities to integrate and support their other interests; they may ask questions about psychic topics, but unless this aspect is reinforced, these abilities may disappear totally. The child will not normally allow that aspect to dominate.

If anything, because of their wide and inspired interests, the multiply gifted child will appear a little wasteful of their energies.

Their inquisitiveness will drive them through a whole scattering of subjects that fascinate them. Yet these children seem to take, intuitively, the right course in letting their psychic talents underwrite their interests without an insistence on making those talents prominent.

It is not unusual for them to be the first to recognize the contemptuous manner in which psychic questions are treated in the society around them. It may not even be apparent to the family that the child is using psychic perceptions to underwrite other developing interests.

If the parents are in a position to answer a child's questions about the psychic experience, it will be all to the child's good.

As children, they are most likely *not* to seek to make their psychic gift preeminent over other talents unless encouraged to do so.

They will be more interested in consuming a myriad of information.

In fact, the psychic elements may naturally recede completely: children may end up using them only unconsciously as sources of creative or inventive intuition when, as adults, they have selected a particular field of interest.

They will probably go through several fields of interest before, as teen-agers or young adults, they settle for one.

As adults, few of these Renaissance children will deliberately select out the psychic arts, or some aspect of them for specific development. Nonetheless some of the most noted psychics in the world, have come from the ranks of the multiply gifted.[3]

---

[3] Ingo left no notes or indication as to whom he was referring to, however, he often regarded Edgar Cayce and Harold Sherman with great adoration. A more complete list of famous psychics may be found at PsychicScience.org/psychics.

GIFTED
IN A SPECIFIC WAY

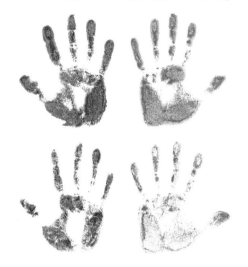

he psychically gifted child may become an active child psychic in this specific way: one aspect of the child's psychic awareness will have become so pronounced and exceptional that the child's attention will have become fixated upon it.

This development may be very dramatic. It will certainly be so for the parents and immediate family, who will likely suffer all sorts of bewilderments if they are unprepared to deal with it.

Somewhat the same situation can arise for adults who suddenly recover something of their psychic potential. Although as adults, they will have a far larger frame of reference within which to work than they did as young children.

In talking about the exceptional specific gift, we are truly talking about genius, and its manifestations can be quite shocking to the sensibilities.

The specifically gifted psychic child suffers most from any *less than understanding* responses from the people around them. If the child's environment is dramatically anti-psychic, the emotional strain on the child will be quite severe.

No one really knows how to cope with this type of child, and the family is often ultimately pressed into seeking professional help.

Considering the anti-psychic stance of most professionals, whatever help they can give, will not be enough. In addition to all this, probably because of the one-sided nature of the initial psychic development, the child may demonstrate serious deficiencies or lack of balance in many other aspects of the child's personality.

Except for the fact that their specific gift is one of a psychic nature, they fall clearly among the group of children who, very early, exhibit specific superlative abilities in art, music, literature, or mathematics.

They are over-imaginative, over-emotional, and, as might be expected in the case of specific psychic giftedness, hypersensitive. Sometimes they are clumsy and physically weak. They can be impractical and absentminded.

Their psychic giftedness is, as a result, generally neither understood nor appreciated by parents and teachers, and among their peers they are likely to be the targets of ridicule and antagonism.

When this is the case – as, unfortunately, it often is – the child will almost be forced to introvert, with disastrous consequences, and much despair and despondency.

The psychic drive that began before the child's birth and quickly crystalized into a definite psychic talent, will by this time, have been totally thwarted, and the revolt going on in the child's inner life will lead to ominous personality changes. Yet even if the parents, peers and environment are perfectly pro-psychic, another terrible phenomenon can occur.

The adults, recognizing the child's special gift, will sometimes seek to force its cultivation, with the aim of producing a child psychic prodigy. If they do this without taking into consideration the consequences of such a lopsided development, the child may well end up in the same condition as the victim of a fiercely anti-psychic environment.

PART **FIVE**

"Young heads take example of the ancient."

-- QUEEN ELIZABETH I

THE WORST THING
TO DO
IF THE CHILD TURNS PSYCHIC

I f the parent suddenly becomes aware that the child is manifesting psychic tendencies, the worst thing to do is to expect the worst.

The worst is not going to happen.

A lot of horror stories have circulated, novels have been written and movies produced that portray the psychic child as an unpredictable monster with powerful abilities who uses them in obscene ways. *This is all fiction.*

Unfortunately, most of us have allowed fiction to shape our expectations to a larger degree than we would like to admit.

The psychic child is not a potential monster. The psychic child is, on the contrary, a fragile being filled with innocent love, seeking to learn and to verify their own experience.

The parents may well be startled, but only because they have not included in their own learning anything about the real nature of the psychic realms.

All of the literature about real psychic experiences indicate that the psychic realms are *rather beautiful*.

The psychic sensitivities of the child might lead them into an encounter with something scary – such as darkness, or some negative telepathic thought – but the volatile reactions of frightened parents will scare them much more.

THE BEST THING TO DO
IF THE CHILD TURNS PSYCHIC

If the parents begin to suspect the child is showing some signs of being psychic, the best thing to do first is to come to terms with their own reactions.

There are today more sources of psychic knowledge available than ever before. Many of them require long-term reading and study, and in some of them the basic issues may not be clear. However in the long run, parents can, with a little effort, develop an overview about the nature of *psychicness* and its creative promise.

The innate psychic sensitivities of the child can be reduced to a "wreck" in no time if the parents subject the child to misunderstandings and over emotional responses.

The small psychic child has no idea at all that they are doing something different when the child gives evidence of their developing psychic nature. To the child, the experiences involved will be as real as anything else the child is experiencing.

If the telepathic bonding with the parents is strong – which it probably is – the child will quickly begin to sense the parents' confusion, and begin the process of withdrawal from them, at least along psychic lines.

If the parents quickly come to terms with their own reactions, then they will be able to enter into a simple creative dialogue with the child – one that is at least free of fear or outrage.

If the child continues to bloom psychically in proportion to how the child grows in other ways, what follows then can only be a delight. The reward will be a deep family closeness.

WORK WITH,
NOT AGAINST
THE PSYCHIC CHILD

L earning to work with the psychic child requires not only a little tact, but also a willingness on the parents' part to be led by the child, to a certain degree.

The child is, after all, closer to and more intimate with the psychic level than the parents who may have lost all their own psychic awareness.

Given support and reinforcement, the psychic child will evolve naturally to some degree. The child's own psychic nature will only become problematical with the realization that being psychic invokes problems in the environment around them.

If parents and teachers realize that the child's psychic processes are innate processes – even though their origin is not understood – they can easily understand that the psychic processes have a reason for existing, much the same as do other innate processes the child possesses.

Admittedly, it is something of a problem to learn to work with something that we don't really know how to work with. Real knowledge only comes from experience. So the parent or the teacher must be willing to experience along with the psychic child, in order to learn how to work with them.

It is important to learn to identify the preliminary phenomena that indicates the child is participating in the psychic level – and that this level is surfacing along with other intellectual capabilities.

This kind of phenomenon is, I think, easy to recognize.

The child cries when the parents are sad or are fighting; the child is joyful when the parents are.

The observant parents can quickly learn to associate their moods with the discomfort of the child. The emotions are flowing along the lines of the telepathic bonding.

The psychic awareness of the average psychic child might not develop much past this stage.

However if any of the psychic processes do begin to crystallize into more obvious abilities or talents, the child will start trying to talk about them or act them out while at play. When this happens, it only means that psychic perceptions are entering the child's consciousness and beginning to take up some intellectual learning time.

Any first steps toward learning how to work with the psychic child must begin with the parents, the immediate family, and a little later on, teachers.

One of the first things to realize is that if a child is showing signs of an inherent psychic nature, the child will not be aware that they are doing anything different from what is expected.

The child will try to talk about what they are experiencing as if the experiences are part of a natural world for them.

The child's inherent psychic nature will become difficult and more so when they discover that their parents are responding in ways that imply the child is wrong in experiencing what is being experienced.

If we bear in mind that telepathic bonding between mother and child probably continues in a robust condition well after birth, it is probable that the child will sense the mother's inner responses to its own emerging psychic experiences.

If the mother's response is alarm, even though the mother keeps a straight face, the child may well sense the unease.

If the child's telepathic state is very pronounced, their telepathic awareness will extend into the environment and can quite possibly include the entire family unit.

All of the evidence for telepathy that I have studied clearly indicates that telepathy and emotions are very closely associated.

While psychology recognizes emotional bonding as having a reality, the close connection between emotional bonding and telepathic bonding is not nearly so well recognized.

Emotions and telepathy are notoriously nonlogical: both are experienced rather than thought about. Science, relying exclusively on logic, will be of little help in coming to grips with factors that are not amenable to logic.

If the parents' responses to the child's psychic manifestations are negative, it is probable that the child will, to some degree, echo their reactions. The parents, feeling that the child has suddenly grown uncanny, may experience a whole gamut of strange emotions: sudden fear, revulsion, suspicion, all with an automatic feeling of wanting to put a distance between them and the source of the uncanniness. These emotions may be picked up telepathically by the child, with obvious repercussions.

Parents' first step, then, in addition to studying the information contained in this book, is to educate themselves, to become familiar with the concept of the psychic universe and what it includes, so that their automatic emotional responses can take on a more stable character.

In our culture, unfortunately, what the psychic universe actually includes is not very well understood.

Parapsychology has intellectualized psychic talents far too much, when in fact psychic talents of any kind are much more experiences than they are intellectualizations.

Excellent sources of education are books written by psychics, especially those containing passages that describe their authors' own psychic childhood experiences. The best source of all however will be the child themselves.

The parents should be prepared to put aside their preconceptions and take the time to find out actually what is happening in the child's mind. It may be only a little, or it may be a great deal. By doing this, the parents then can gear their responses to the needs of the child, and begin to work with them.

KEEP IT SIMPLE

$\mathscr{C}$hildren have attention spans of different lengths. The child's intellectual attention span is quite short, whereas that of the child's emotions is very large.

In contrast, the child's psychic attention span is neither short nor long: it can be best described as pervasive. That is to say, it exists all the time, and permeates the environment around the child.

Our present culture, and the English language, contain no words to express the child's psychic components. And so the child will never learn them.

If the child's psychic nature is pronounced, the child will, however, invent words or mixtures of words that – to them – carry the right meaning.

These little words might sound, to the parents, like gibberish, similar to the unrecognizable little drawings that children do.

Like the drawings, the words carry meanings, and relationships of meanings, that are important to the child.

For example, a little boy once said to his father: "Daddy, you got lots of butterfly-drops." The father had no idea what "butterfly-drops" referred to, and when he asked the child to further describe them, the child could not.

At times the child would go into sort of a daydreaming state, and when asked what he was thinking about, he replied, "Butterfly-drops."

The parents, who were friends of mine, asked me if in my career as an artist I had ever come across a symbolic meaning for butterfly-drops. I said no, but suggested that they ask the child to make a drawing. He drew a pretty good figure representing his father, with a lot of little dots around it. These dots, he said, were butterfly-drops.

It became clear then that butterfly had to do with butterfly wings, which the child already knew represented scintillating colors and that butterfly-drops referred to the father's aura. When the child was asked if he was referring to the colors around his father, he launched into a veritable discourse: "Oh, yes, and sometimes the butterflies are red and sometimes yellow, and they fly around, just like lots of butterflies, and sometimes there are snakes, too, but I don't like those."

A more wonderful description of the body's energy fields could hardly have been obtained. This was also the first clue the parents had that their son was experiencing non-sensory perceptions. They were quite surprised and became interested in the subject. They took the initiative to try to preserve their son's psychic potential and have been quite successful.

They developed a very workable approach. I suggested that the child be encouraged to portray his non-sensory perceptions through simple drawings, and not so much through words, so that the parents could see something of what the child otherwise could not convey verbally.

They kept it all very simple, answering the child's questions with brief responses gauged to match his intellectual attention span.

That emotional support from the parents eventually allowed the child to gain a healthy perspective about it all. Eventually, he himself volunteered the fact that most other kids could not perceive butterfly-drops because, as he put it, "they didn't want to."

He worked out the social implications without much assistance from his parents – who naturally were fascinated. "I guess I can't talk to them about this...." And in that way, the child passed with hardly any emotional damage to himself, through the crisis of meeting rejection about psychic matters.

Today he is ten, and when asked, he can talk about bodies and their energies – as he says: "Dark energy seems to mean the person is going to get the flu and lots of light energy mostly means the kid is going to be a good soccer player."

Thus, this child is continuing, at his own personal level, to integrate his special gift into his life as his life develops.

PART **SIX**

"I dwell in possibility..."

-- **EMILY DICKINSON**

TRANS
FORMATIONS

he child is headed for a series of natural transformations that will govern the child's life.

In the biological sense, these transformations are predetermined. Birth is the first biological event that places the little machine, and the human entity in it, into the outer universe.

The little machine quickly undergoes a series of biological and mental transformations that are reflected not only in its outer growth, but by the astonishing complexity of its thinking apparatus.

The course of these transformations is not always placid, as any experienced parent knows.

But if the parent is prepared in advance to recognize the signs and characteristics of these great changes, the duress they bring can be better tolerated.

If it is understood that the child's psychic nature is a key aspect of mental transformations, then it is easy also to understand that the psychic nature will take its natural place among the child's other developing mental attributes – providing the child's psychic manifestations are not too grossly reproved by the child's parents or others around the child.

Even where the child's psychic abilities are obvious, the psychic universe will probably submerge naturally as the child's interest in the complexities of the outer world increases. There, these abilities will perform their natural function as a tool that aids intuition and creativity.

If the child's psychic universe has been well tended by the parents, it will exist in a healthy, robust form. If this universe has been victimized by negative reactions during its early formation, it may submerge in some aberrated form, or attenuate completely.

I think we have, by now, come to realize the importance that the child's psychic awarenesses occupy in helping to form the child's total personality.

The transforming potentials of the child's psychic experiences should not be minimized. The child's psychic awarenesses – whether they are conscious or unconscious – clearly aid even in those transformations that are not pronounced enough to produce a clear, identifiable psychic talent.

We have seen how closely connected to the child's psychic awarenesses must be the valuable abilities of intuition, creativity, and telepathic bonding.

The child's psychic nature acts as a transforming agent in all three of these very important areas.

THE PSYCHIC CHILD
BECOMES ACTIVE

If the child is gifted with a pronounced psychic nature, this nature can very well become quite active. As soon as the child has a sufficient vocabulary, the child will begin talking about it and eventually ask questions about it.

Indeed, it is probably at this point that the parents, if they have not recognized the child's psychic aptitudes before, will come face-to-face with them. For example, out of the blue, the child can suddenly ask:

"Daddy, what is that light around your body?"

"Mummy, why were you thinking that thought?"

"Granny, my little invisible friend is saying hello to you, why don't you answer?"

These kinds of questions often stun those to

whom they are addressed. The average response is to freeze up altogether; the second most likely is to ask the child what the child means.

If the child can answer, they will now come out with descriptions of their psychic world that further perplex the adult. In most cases, the adult will assume that the child has suddenly become abnormal, and there will ensue a rush to return them to normality, with measures extending from merely calling the child silly to taking punitive actions if the child persists.

Many children accept this, because they do learn very early that several areas of interest are forbidden them anyway. Anything that either embarrasses the parents' moral attitudes or raises questions the parents cannot deal with is likely to be a forbidden topic.

The precocious psychic child, however, might very well resist any forceful invalidation of their psychic experiences, just as any other child would who is gifted with precocious talents. The parent who is best equipped by informed expectation will be the best able to deal with the psychic issues, if they arise.

They are actually easy to deal with.

The child is only seeking information when asking questions. And, most importantly, is only passing through a natural stage of their psychic development.

The way parents respond creatively to the child has to be left up to them, but generally, because children's attention spans are relatively short, short answers are probably best.

The drawings of a child are very revealing. They show that the child is thinking of things, in meaning-sense, long before they can accurately draw or sketch the visual attributes of, say, a man or a house.

For example, the child draws a circle. When asked what it is, the child says it is Mommie. But the circle also has a wobbly line protruding from of it. When asked what that is, the child says that it's Mommie's thoughts.

The parents who tells the child that Mommie doesn't look like that and that her thoughts are, anyway, inside her head, has missed the point.

I've actually seen a drawing made by a little girl about three and a half years old. It showed two upright stick figures with no heads but connected by a curved line going between the two. The little girl stated that the first stick was her mother, and the second was herself, and the curved line was her mother's thoughts getting over to her.

This sketch was, of course, a very adequate example coming *from the child* of the telepathic bonding between herself and her mother.

To tell the child that thoughts don't do that only contributes to the destruction of the bond, and it is not clear at all that there is any wisdom in telling a child such a thing. Fortunately, the mother who showed this drawing to me was an informed mother and instantly recognized the meaning of the drawing for what it was.

When the mother asked the daughter if she wanted to talk about this, the little daughter replied, "Mommie, what's there to talk about?" Today that child is thirteen years old, and has developed quite differently from the mother; yet there is between them a very loving and peaceful relationship. The daughter's psychic nature seems pronounced, but it is not at all exaggerated or neurotic.

THE OUT-OF-BODY
PSYCHIC CHILD

Nothing is more shocking for parents than to find their little child pensive or moody one day and, when asked why the child replies with something like "I saw myself last night. I was up by the ceiling...." Followed perhaps by a series of questions:

"Daddy, can you do it, too?"

"Do what?"

"Go through the wall."

The out-of-body experience is, of course, a prime psychic experience. Nevertheless, it is one whose reality has been hotly contested, and psychologists have offered many reasons by which it can be explained away.

Attitudes about the out-of-body experience have changed during the fifteen years I have been an active participant in parapsychological research. The primary reason for this change has been, I think, the widespread interest in the clinical death experience, instances during which a person is clinically dead for a short time, but recovers, to everyone's astonishment.

These people very often report having been outside their body, moving down hospital corridors, or rising into the sky. They can see everything very well, but no one can see them. They report being transparent, and other people at the scene just walk right through them.

They often meet and see loved ones and friends who have died, and in some cases beings who are angelic and saintly.

There are other famous cases in which individuals got outside their bodies while anesthetized during operations. Many soldiers mortally wounded during battle often report this kind of experience.

The transforming nature of this kind of psychic experience is almost always very pronounced. The person who experiences it sees life from a totally new point of view – one that implies immortality and bestows upon the individual a sublime peacefulness that they may never have experienced before.

This kind of psychic experience is not unusual in the case of the psychic child, especially if the child is among the gifted or super-gifted.

Among the many types of psychic giftedness, it is perhaps the only one that, of itself, can cause problems for the child.

In rare cases the child can temporarily confuse the center of their physical senses with their out-of-body perceptions.

Having two centers of perception can become a temporary problem, arousing a lot of questions that are difficult to answer.

While out-of-body, the child-being can encounter many things in life that are unfamiliar to them, and therefore seem threatening.

On the other hand, the child more often shows none of these darker experiences, and to them the experience is one of joy, liberation, and beauty.

Needless to say, the reactions of the parents are of primary importance.

Here the child needs love and understanding and, above all, the opportunity to have a simple dialogue with their parents. The child did not bring this on themselves. It just happened to them. However parents can be assured that it is a very meaningful experience to the child. Of important note, family induced trauma can convert this sublime experience into one of pain.

One of my coworkers told me of an event of this kind with his own child. The out-of-body state came to their attention – again through a drawing the child had made in school. The child had drawn two small figures. When the teacher asked what they were, the child pointed to one and said that it was himself.

When asked about the other, he said that it was himself also.

The teacher then told him that he could not be in two places at once. To the teacher's surprise, the child burst into tears and protested, "I was so!"

The child's father was a parapsychologist, and began a dialogue with the little tot, only to discover that this situation had been going on for quite some time.

Once the child was drawn out, he himself

finally offered the conclusion that "others can't do it, can they, Daddy?" And balance was restored, simply through a rational discussion.

Here, as with so many other items of interest to the child, he was only seeking the meaning of his experiences and the relationships among them.

Once he had established them, he seemed to integrate his out-of-body experiences quite well. As he grew, they seemed to disappear. The boy was apparently super-gifted in many other areas, especially in languages and the game of chess.

The parents who find their child has out-of-body experiences might just as well get ready to hang on to the seat for a while. They are embarked on a ride through strange territory.

But, given love, the opportunity for dialogue, and frank, open answers to the child's questions, the child will work out the details, and out-of-body potentials will take their natural place among the child's other aptitudes.

PART SEVEN

"The most beautiful thing we can experience is the mysterious."

-- ALBERT EINSTEIN

THE IMPORTANCE
OF A CHILD'S QUEST FOR MEANING

L ong before the child can react intellectually, the child is busy trying to be aware of meanings and relationships.

This is clearly revealed by the child's drawings. Such drawings are not accurate renderings of things, if they are judged by adult standards – which they should never be. They consist of squiggles, misshapen figures, etc. But the smallest of these squiggles has a particular meaning to the child; the child put it there because it conveys a meaning.

When asked what it means, the child can sometimes tell you.

When the child says they don't know, this does not particularly signify that the child   really doesn't know, but more likely that the child doesn't yet have a form of speech to go with the meaning they are trying to convey.

The child's quest for meanings and relationships is often a preverbal affair. It is a combination of the astonishing developments taking place within the child and their developing intellectual potentials.

Only later does the child learn to attach proper words to the meanings and relationships.

The child's own natural internal development will allow for them to make adequate common-sense connections between meanings, but only providing that meanings and relationships have not been made excessively confused.

The parents are often the source of this kind of confusion. If they refuse, or are unable to respond creatively to certain of their child's efforts at achieving understanding, or reject the child's initial attempts to convey meanings, then it is reasonable to assume that the child will grow confused and might stay confused.

Confusion is always painful, and because there is hardly any one area in life that is not somehow related to others, the confusion tends to spread. The child is likely to close down permanently, the awareness of the confused areas in their mind, causing them to atrophy.

For example, if an intellectually gifted or super-gifted child is born into a family of intellectual clods, it is easy to understand that the child's own natural high-stage powers are going to suffer.

The same will be true for the precocious psychically gifted child. Such a child will reach a point very early in the child's young life when the psychic content of the search for meanings and relationships will appear through drawings or though attempts at verbalization. If the child does not find approval and creative support, the child will become confused about psychic experiences and will eventually try to close them down.

We know that many children do this successfully to some degree. But if we consider that the psychic level is part and parcel of the child's basic makeup, then we must also assume that if the child tries to close it down, many natural internal functions will atrophy.

If the child is one who is highly gifted or super-gifted psychically, any confusions the child suffers regarding this talent will not be minor disasters for them: they will be major mental earthquakes.

The gifted child whose talents have been suppressed for one reason or another is often a pathetic sight. Even if the child ultimately manages to reclaim some of the child's talent through willpower and study, the talent will nevertheless often be expressed through the neuroses brought on by the mockery or hostility of the child's parents and peers.

The growing child, will eventually, find reservoirs of support outside the uncooperative family unit if the child's talents lie in fields already encouraged by society – the arts, literature, science, invention, and so on.

But this will not likely be true of psychic abilities, which are, for the most part, rejected by society.[4]

The tiny child will not reach these until the

---

[4] However, the trend to incorporate psychic studies into the child's educational system shows signs of beginning, though, as a few schools have installed basic parapsychology courses.

child grows up a little.

By that age, if the family unit was unprepared to preserve and conserve them, the child's psychic abilities may have manifested and be destroyed.

PART **EIGHT**

"When I used to read fairy tales, I fancied
that kind of thing never happened, and now
here I am in the middle of one!"

-- CHAPTER 4, ALICE'S ADVENTURES IN WONDERLAND, BY LEWIS CARROLL

THE PSYCHIC CHILD'S
SENSE OF BELONGING

If the psychic child's emerging psychic nature is denied or ridiculed, the child may take one of two paths.

The child can make the decision that one's psychic nature does not belong in that world that is denying or criticizing it. The average child can, and most likely will, lose interest in this aspect of themselves, and repress it.

If the child is gifted or super-gifted, and the child's psychic awarenesses are highly acute, the child may not readily accept denial or ridicule. Little children can be very obstinate in seeking basic meanings and relationships. If the child dearly perceives their psychic world, denial of it and ridicule of their questions will be hard for the child to accept.

The child may take to feeling that the child does not belong in the world from which the denial and ridicule is emanating, and introvert into the child's psychic world.

The gifted child who is forced, between the tender ages of three and six, into themselves is truly unfortunate, and can be expected to suffer the aberrations associated with loneliness.

Here the parents face a particularly difficult and noble task, one both exacting and difficult. If unable to cope, they will need the help of competent advisors.

But whether the task falls to the parents or their advisers, the goal must be the same. The child needs to be helped to distribute the child's sense of belonging between the outer world of life and the child's internal psychic experiences.

This needs to be done in proportion to the child's manifest psychic awarenesses and gifts – in the expectation that the psychic gifts will eventually integrate with the child's other interests when these are restored.

If this is done with delicacy and wisdom, the child will come to accept that while their psychic gifts belong to them, they in turn belong in the family and ultimately in the outer world toward which the child is headed anyway.

Often what the child needs is association with other children with similar natures, to find mutual support and interests, in a psychic-spiritual sense, and share a sense of belonging.

The company of "normal" children does not satisfy them – it often has, in fact, an adverse effect. The "normal" ones cannot understand or appreciate the gifted psychic child, and are as likely as not to turn hostile.

Children have amazing powers of recovery if provided avenues that allow them some support. Particular attention should be given to developing a child's pride in their psychic giftedness, balanced with support for the child's natural wish to belong to the normal world around them.

THE PSYCHIC CHILD'S
SENSE OF THE INFINITE

Super-gifted psychic children show an interest in deep philosophical and spiritual subjects at a very early age.

Their psychic nature places them in contact with large, invisible issues that may totally escape other children and even some adults. Such children very often possess real intuition and spiritual illumination.

Real and valuable intuitions are part of their above-average psychic makeup, while their spiritual illuminations result from meanings that have come to them as a result of their super-awarenesses.

Researchers have observed that children, even at ages five to seven, are interested in the problems of the origin and destiny of man and ask precise questions about life and death.

This kind of interest – as might be expected – can be particularly pronounced in the psychic child. In fact, if the child has not already demonstrated some other kind of psychic awareness, such questions might be the first factors to alert the parents that the child is processing information at a deep psychic, intuitive level.

All children have the right to have their questions taken seriously and to receive adequate answers.

But these answers must be based upon two factors:

- the parents or teachers must be capable of dealing with them; and,
- they must deal with them at a level that is reasonable to the child's stage of interest and speed of learning.

This is sometimes hard to do, because adults may not have settled in their own minds the issues involved.

In fact, the psychic issue may be one of the areas "forbidden" to family discussions.

If we accept the idea that a particular psychic child's telepathic bonding is not submerging, but in fact is enlarging to include other psychic awarenesses, outside the relationship between the child and the parents, then we must also assume that the child is trying to establish logical meanings for the universals with which the child is in increasing contact.

One thing often overlooked is that if the child has already organized awareness so that the child can ask a question about one of these deep philosophical or spiritual issues, it is more than likely that the child already has made some decision about it, or at least some nucleus of a decision.

In asking the question, the child is only seeking approval for a decision the child has already taken.

It is exactly in the area of philosophical or spiritual values that the parents frequently wish to mold the child in their own image.

Perceptive child psychologists have doubted the efficacy of this approach for two reasons. First, the adult responses – based on their own values – might not truly address the questions the child has asked; and second, the child's philosophical and spiritual needs are going to be fulfilled from a multitude of sources.

If the adult responses do not fit well with the child's own awarenesses, the child may ultimately reject the values of the child's parents and family. This situation can be particularly pronounced in the case of a super-gifted psychic child, because probably the child's psychic levels of awareness are already delivering the child information that might contrast sharply with the philosophical and spiritual values of the parents.

The child might appear to accept pat answers, but will not in fact do so. A true dialogue is needed based upon the understanding that the psychic child's essential values are at stake.

Since the child may already have made a decision concerning the subject being asked about, it would be a creative step to try finding out what that decision was, and what led up to it.

If the child has gained confidence that the child can discuss these kinds of issues without fear of being made to look foolish, this is the moment when their natural intuitions can blaze forth with extraordinary brilliance, even if they're expressed in the small terms available to a child.

Parents who wish to preserve their child's psychic nature must observe and encourage all spontaneous manifestations of a spiritual awareness, with all the intuitions, illuminations, and aspirations associated with them.

No parapsychological or psychic sensitivities the child might demonstrate should be ridiculed or denied. They should be explained as far as possible, in terms the child can understand, within the limits of their attention span.

Once a working relationship is achieved between the psychic child and the parent-teacher, the manifestations can be carefully watched and regulated.

PART **NINE**

"The beginning is always today."

-- MARY SHELLEY

THREE TYPES
OF EDUCATION THAT ARE NECESSARY FOR THE PSYCHIC CHILD

We have now seen that many different factors must go into preserving the child's psychic nature.

And we have seen that there are many different types of psychic children.

There is the "average" child whose psychic nature never becomes visible and submerges quickly after birth. At the other end of the spectrum is the psychically super-gifted child who demonstrates pronounced psychic abilities and is intellectually interested in them.

If the child is only minimally gifted, showing few signs of psychic potential, it would be wise perhaps to help the child raise their psychic threshold a little – to guide the child to a slightly greater awareness about this important gift.

But it is probably never wise to force the gifted psychic child to lower their psychic awarenesses, any more than it is to try to decrease any manifestations of a giftedness in a child.

Children of all types should be supported, and given the nourishment appropriate to their individual growth patterns.

If the family unit is unable to do this, then it should seek outside knowledge and help.

There are three types of education the family unit can provide for their psychic child: physical education, imagination training, and support for the child's developing intelligence.

The child actually needs experience in all of these areas to help the child achieve the balance necessary for them in life.

PHYSICAL EDUCATION

FOR THE PSYCHIC CHILD

The mental and imaginative qualities of the psychic child are often excessive. As such, the child needs a productive program of physical education to help the child even out the child's contact with the rest of life. In this, the child is not much different from other types of gifted or super-gifted children.

Run-of-the-mill sports programs generally prove ill-suited to the psychic child. Unless the child shows an interest in competitive types of physical education sports, such activities will not solve the problem.

Gifted children are usually not interested in them anyway, and forcing them to compete often serves merely to subject them to the ridicule of other children more vigorously enthusiastic.

The psychic child will appreciate much more, a direct and prolonged contact with nature: camping, hiking, nature walks, and activities in the wild that encourage the child to call upon their natural intuitions.

In fact, exposure to nature might act as therapy for psychic children who may have already started to introvert before the exact characterization of their situation can be divined.

Psychic children are also fascinated by living things, at least when they are very small, and enjoy playing with them. Even when very young, psychic children are likely to develop an interest in gardening and the raising of small animals. Activities of this sort help the child learn by doing, and provide further means to develop their psychic awareness.

Even the youngest psychic child will be mesmerized by nature, even if it is so tiny that the child can only watch it.

THE PSYCHIC CHILD'S
IMAGINATION

I magination is one of the greatest of human gifts.

Children are taught to imagine all sorts of things, whether from fairy tales or from games of "let's pretend."

Imagination, though, is a special problem with psychically gifted children, because it is hard to tell the difference between it and their real psychic attributes.

It is difficult for the parents, but it will also become so for the child – unless the child is educated by slow degrees to discriminate between the products of their imagination and those of real psychic experience or awareness.

The surest way to destroy the gifts of very young psychic children is to accuse them of simply having vivid imaginations, while at the same time encouraging them to lose themselves in fairy tales and "let's pretend" games.

Both imagination and psychic awareness are precision functions, and they have far more importance than is generally recognized. All high-stage creativity in the adult, or even in the teenager, has as its basis, imagination and psychic awareness.

Super-gifted children, notably in particular, have overactive imaginations, and it is important for them to be helped, at a very early age, not to close down their imagination, but to be able to tell the difference between it and real psychic signals.

The child's imaginary world will, as they mature, have to be sublimated or turned into constructive use.

At the same time, the psychic child's innate gifts must be enhanced if they are to be preserved.

Given support, the child will soon be able to tell the difference between their own imagination and their psychic experience. The best way to help the child do so is to increase the child's awareness of what is imaginary through exercises to help them determine whether the results are due to/from their imagination or actual psychic experience.

GUIDING
THE PSYCHIC CHILD'S
INTELLIGENCE

The psychically aware child will probably also be a child of wide interests.

It won't be long before the child starts resenting an education based on rote learning and memorization – methods that do not promote the training and use of the mind.

Even while very young, the super-gifted psychic child will initiate a wide spectrum of inquiry on their own. By the time the child is six or seven, the child may well have out-distanced others of similar age in pure consumption of intellectual learning.

Materials about our psychic nature need to be provided to these children, though couched in terms they can deal with. Often just the satisfaction of learning, even a minimum, about psychic things helps to stabilize their confidence.

Like other super-gifted children, the psychic child feels a great need to learn, and as soon as the child can do so, the child is likely to start consuming encyclopedias and dictionaries.

Often the child will go about it without any particular pattern that the parents can discover, in spurts and starts that reflect nothing more than the length of the child's attention span.

Almost anything that will help flatter the child's mental dexterity – and the child's manual dexterity as well – is desirable.

The psychic child, especially when the child is young, will begin to alternate periods of intellectual interest with play and periods of reflection.

In fact, the psychic child is normally highly reflective, quietly observing all things in great detail.

A PRÉCIS

"The psychic child is actually a thing of beauty and joy and promise."

-- INGO SWANN

A SUMMARY
OF HOW TO ACT TOWARD A PSYCHIC CHILD

elping and guiding a psychic child is an art that requires common sense.

Common sense is very important, but to be effective, it must be based upon sufficient information.

Effective help and guidance for the psychic child lets the child integrate the psychic aspects with the other parts of the child's life.

If you want to learn to deal with a psychic child, common sense suggests the first step you should take.

All the other steps follow from that first step. It is important to learn what is known about extrasensory perception and other psychic gifts, so that you can:

- Control your own responses and reactions to your child if asked a question about psychic matters or if the child suddenly demonstrates a psychic trait.
- Generally let the child take the initiative, and don't try to force upon the child your own preconceptions.
- Keep the interchanges short and at a language level the child can understand.
- Answer the child's questions fairly and honestly.
- Praise the child when psychic experiences are arousing enthusiasm and interest.

- Give the child other kinds of support if experiences are making the child sad or confused, and try to explain what you think may be happening to them.
- Always ask the child what their drawings mean to them, and how their psychic content fits in with other aspects of their life.
- Ask the child to draw out what they mean so you have a chance of understanding the child better if the child uses gibberish words.
- Never deride or react angrily toward the delicate psychic child.
- Keep your dialogue short as the child's intellectual attention span will be short.
- Make your love and understanding a permanent part of your relationship toward them as the child's emotional involvement may be longer.
- Try to use your telepathic bonding to intuit what may be taking place if the child acts withdrawn about something you think may be psychic in origin.
- Point out if the child's sensitivity starts contributing to the child's creativity or knowledge, and reinforce it with a quick, helpful dialogue.
- Help the child to understand their world better, but also suggest additional interests that will help the child achieve balance, if the psychic child becomes active in some specific talent.
- Never force the psychic child to be psychic if the child doesn't want to be.
- Try to find other children of approximately the same temperament for your child to socialize with.

- Meet with other parents in a similar situation and with similar goals for the psychic support of their children to share and compare experiences.
- Understand that the child will go through several phases until the child arrives at a comfortable tolerance for their own awarenesses.
- Help them to understand the reasons should the child meet with conflict or derision outside the family unit or among their peers.
- Be prepared for surprises and be able to share in the child's joy as the child reaches each new level of understanding.

BACK MATTER

"This is a brief life, but in its brevity it offers us some splendid moments, some meaningful adventures."

-- RUDYARD KIPLING

CLOSING THOUGHTS

Now that the years let me look back, and now that I have a larger intellectual vantage point from which to examine my life and develop an understanding of psychic processes, my own psychic childhood has more meaning than ever. I can see how I must have mystified my family, seeing and talking about things they couldn't see.

My maternal grandmother was my strongest supporter. She was intensely intuitive in a simple and direct way. She, too, so she said, had been a psychic child.

I've lived what seems to me at time a hard life with many dark moments. But my early psychic awareness never really left me, even though it did submerge for many years.

My psychic awareness also preserved for me a love for beauty in a world today transfixed by ugliness and it reemerged at last because of my association with parapsychology experiments.

I began to study psychic matters, and to see how closely they are associated not only with psychic feats, but with creativity; how they permitted a better understanding of the invisible energies upon which creativity is founded. For it is love that creates the psychic energy that sponsors survival.

I believe that the *Déjà vu* experience is real, something that takes place, most probably, in us while we sleep. Not a dream, but an actual event that happens to us when part of us enters the time stream in an out-of-body state during sleep. If we remember these events when we wake, we tend to interpret them as dreams, for our culture is not trained in discriminating among the many different kinds of sleep phenomena. But for the most part, we remember them not at all, and only upon occasion encounter an event or place that seems familiar to us.

I don't believe that we totally lose our innate psychic awarenesses. My own intuitions saved my life twice as a child, once in Korea, and four times in the difficult city of New York.

All of these together and many, many more point to the fact that there is a universe of some kind beyond the one we normally call rational, a universe that is being investigated by advanced quantum physicists even as I write this. It is known that in this strange and "irrational" universe, time and space disobey the laws they follow in the physical universe: it is also known that the human mind possesses strange "irrational" powers concerning time and space.

For me, I have been able, through these awarenesses, to contact to my greater self, and I believe that it is only through psychic awareness that this can be done; no one really understands oneself unless one can put one's own psychic potentials to use in the search for this understanding.

***

A BioMind
Superpowers Book
from
Swann-Ryder
Productions, LLC

www.ingoswann.com

Made in the USA
Middletown, DE
27 November 2021